Passion

Poetry and Poetry Therapy:
Selected writings in Poetry and Psychology on Self-development

Second Edition

Elaine H. Olaoye, Ph.D.

Northwind Publishers
Red Bank, New Jersey
2002

Copyright © 2002 Elaine Henry Olaoye

All rights reserved
No portion of this book may be reproduced in any form without written permission from the publisher.

Second Edition
Second Printing

Library of Congress Catalog Card Number 98-91450

1. Poetry, 2 .Psychology 3. Self-help
4. Poetry Therapy 5. Affirmations
6. .Afro-Americans

ISBN 1-880764-14-8

Northwind Publishers
Red Bank, New Jersey

Printed in U.S.A.
by Morris Publishing

Introduction to New Editon 2002

Teaching psychology for 25 years and observing the strides made under behaviorism while riding the progress in biology, statistics and technology, one is amazed at the developments made in psychology in the 20th century.

However, after noting some difficulties created by the behavioristic approach, *Passions of the Soul* was introduced as a supplementary text. Students were introduced to two epistemologies: the hypothetico-deductive method used by behaviorism and the metaphorical-abductive method, which teaches how to use the multiple associations and meanings of metaphor to understand the uniqueness, complexities and differences that characterize people.

Students wrote essays comparing treatment of subjects like love, friendship, homeostatis, and attribution theory in both texts. For example, students compared this behavioristic approach to love to relevant poems (p.36-40):

"You take the first step in understanding psychological process by describing it as...objectively as possible. Consider love....Psychologist Zick Rubin says many objective behaviors signify love. For example, one way to tell when two people are in love is to measure how much time they spend looking into each other's eyes (Rubin 1973)...Such behavioral descriptions of an otherwise fuzzy concept, like love is an operational definition. Observatons made of these behaviors become the "facts" of psychology known as data" (Zimbard, et. al. 2000).

The results were dramatic! The energy and interest level of students in three colleges went up significantly. The higher quality and quantity of writing generated evidence in support of this. The 'return of the mind' under cognitive psychology has expanded the domain of psychology. It allows students to participate in a psychology that engages the complexity and creativity of mind and emotions. The poetry in this volume was helpful to students because of the relevance of subject matter to psychology and the accessibility, beauty, brevity and rich associations of the language.

Most important however, was the progress students made as manifested by their ability to evaluate the poetry therapy embodied in the recipes (p.75). In a comparison with cognitive or humanistic therapy and their usefulness in helping with problems in living, students were able to identify the contributions of imagery and the imagination in e.g. 'Love-spiced Cobblers' and 'Bitter Sweet Veggies'. Some students comments follow:

1. "The recipe "Bitter Sweet Veggies is ingenious. Its steps are easy yet affective. By alternating memories of loss with memories of gratitude a grieving person...is enabled to see that life is not all good and not all bad. The poems provide comfort and hope to a person hurting over the loss of a loved one...Compared to humanistic therapies, "Bitter Sweet Veggies" fulfills all of the qualities...It internally uses reflection of feelings by means of the poems..."Bitter Sweet Veggies" is a non-directive recipe because the person wearing the apron can stop anytime."

2. "The poems support the self-help process that must occur in therapy. The "appliances" and "utensils" needed for the recipes described in Passions, are actually metaphors used to describe what is needed for people to practice what is needed for healing. A resilence-coated wooden spoon is a good example of a cognition that is needed for behavior change, resilence being the ability to "bounce-back" from a stressful situation. An imagination-powered microwave oven is appropriate also because imagination can help patients develop ways to cope with their problems...The recipes provide the reader with more ways to use their imaginations which can help them produce mechanisms to possibly prevent bad cognitions and in turn nurture good behavior patterns."

3. "When we are seeking help for emotional confusion...we need to be able to imagine ourselves in a light that is opposite to our current behavior. Imagination is important when using Dr. Olaoye's recipes. We take "cooking and eating" as metaphors and use them to feed our hearts and heads."

Elaine H. Olaoye 2002

N.B.
More students' responses are in the Appendix on page 88.

Passions of the Soul
Introduction

This volume invites each of us to explore our relationship with ourselves and rediscover the hidden pleasures and powers of human life and living.

The poetry draws on the psychological insights that come out of the author's formal training, the rich poetic traditions that span centuries and that are also cultivated in many countries around the world. The nurture and enjoyment of the passionate moments explored in this text can do much to light the emotional fires that in turn warm and illuminate the solitary disciplines of daily living: from the appreciation of visual stimuli and the tingle of tactile senses, to the joy and efflorescence of unimpeded spiritual and melodious flights, or the excitement at the discovery of logical and practical insights.

The full realization of these moments require total engagement: poetry should be allowed to evoke not only images but sounds, memories and music all fueled by underlying feelings. To achieve this, poetry must be read aloud. So each night, in the morning on your lunch or coffee break, read a poem *aloud*, read a poem to the sky! Read one to a co-worker! to a friend, to a supervisor, to a loved one, to oneself. Those that touch you, should be read or played over and over again, so they can imbue your life with their multidimensional possibilities, and help create the colourful jewels and gems that sparkle in the firmament of a reflective life.

Passions of the Soul
Preface

On psychology and poetry in self-development

As a psychologist I am fascinated by the broader role of poetry in human life. The presence of poetry is not only to be found in most cultures around the world, but this literary form dates back to the earlier Western cultures.

Today in an age of skeptics, we tend to appreciate poets more for the questions they raise than the answers they might proffer. We read poetry less to receive some objective truth and more to understand how a particular person struggles to find out what is true for herself. Our expectation that poets admit their subjective focus is paired with another criterion, that poets try to make sense of their experience, that poets use language to clarify and amplify moments of life in a manner that others are likely to find helpful.

Before immersing yourself in the poems gathered together under the rubric "Passions of the Soul", you are invited to pause and dwell on some of the related and common functions of psychology and poetry, to compare, albeit briefly, these two different approaches to acquiring knowledge of the self, the complementary relationship and the necessity of both for personal growth and development.

While scientific psychology begins its official existence in 1879 in Liepzig, Germany, poetry if we take early

Greece as a reference point, goes back at least 2,500 years. Poetry has over this period of time provided a vehicle by which first the acknowledgements of the body, soul and mind, later subsumed under the self, were explored and discovered.

While philosophers from pre-Aristotelian times, but most notably Descartes, struggled with the problem of the existence and relationship of the body, mind and soul, poetry provided the opportunity for this emerging consciousness to express itself.

Today, with much help from psychology we take for granted the self in all its complexity and fragility. The existence of the self in the West, however is a relatively new phenomenon. As Anthony Stort (1988) writes:

The idea that individual self development is an important pursuit is a comparatively recent one in human history and the idea that the arts are vehicles of self-expression or can serve the purpose of self-development is still more recent. At the dawn of history, the arts were strictly functional for the community, not for the individual artist.

The modern meaning of the word *self* as "a permanent subject of successive and varying states of consciousness" according to the *Oxford English Dictionary* was not established until 1674. The concept was introduced as part of a group of compound words such as self-knowledge(1613), self-seeker(1632) and self-hood(1649).(Abbs 1986)

However, the "shift" towards individuation, for which the Renaissance and its artists were celebrated, was a rebirth of a discovery made two thousand years earlier by the early Greek poets. Bruno Snell (1960) recounts that in the two hundred years following Homer, the notions of body and soul had evolved in a manner that allowed them to become complementary parts of a person. The early Greek poets in embracing this were able to begin speaking as individuals instead of only as mere pawns of the gods.

The poets Archilochus, Sappho and Anacreon discovered through their poetry that all people are not striving for the same goals, that each differs in their desires. They also discovered that what was intensely felt was more important than external displays. Sappho, for instance wrote of her love for women even though it was not tolerated by the Church. And each of them in their own way wrote of the distress in their lives which had to be endured but which, if articulated and understood, became a source of comfort. These discoveries charged the imagery of these lyricists with a powerful personal intensity that was unknown until this time.

Peter Abbs (1986) points out that the word *individual* originally signified "indivisible" as in the Christian concept of Trinity, so its meaning as we accept it today represents a gradual shift over time:

*The gradual inversion of meaning for the word individual, moving from the indivisible and collective to the divisible and distinctive, carries quietly within itself the historical development of self consciouness... **that change in structure of feeling which during the Renaissance shifted from a sense of unconscious fusion with the world to a state of conscious individuation..***

While philosophy as the antecedent of psychology provided the analytical tools for formulating an understanding of the evolving structures and relationships of the body, soul and mind, it was poetry that gave the self a viable vehicle for expression and evolution.

Historians have traditionally used technological advances as identifiers of important milestones in a culture. This could be challenged, and the advances in the recognition and evolution of the self might be viewed as the more critical milestones in Western cultural development. Philosophy, poetry and psychology would emerge as major vehicles through which humankind has been able to explore inner space in general as well as provide opportunities for the unfolding of the individuated self.

Currently, scientific psychology with its many areas of subspecialties, in conjunction with other disciplines such as biology, has provided us with a plethora of information about the self: from the various neurotransmitter molecules and the millions of neurons, that physically define the mind as a flow of patterns of billions of neural events, to insights about perception, memory, cognition, development and a wide range of personal and interpersonal behaviors. However, in order to achieve this, psychology has had not only to fragment the self but also to focus on lower levels of functioning.

Poetry, as a result, can continue to complement psychology by being the discipline where individuals can function holistically and also challenge themselves to plumb the depths and reach for the expanding structures of their being. Psychology gives poets new knowledge and insights with which to explore, interpret and articulate their inner worlds. But poets are still responsible for cultivating a sensitivity to themselves and all that is around them and for using language to describe changing identities, to capture meaningfulness, and to rediscover and redefine the self in a postmodern world.

As a psychologist, I mourn the current diminution of the ritual uses of poetry (Vendler 1988) because as historical as well as crosscultural research can show, poetry has played a critical function in integrating and soothing the human mind, body and spirit. Two of the processes by which this happens are: (i) an enhancement of human cognition and (ii) improved coping in reaching emotional resolutions

We can examine an example of the first process as I presented it in an earlier paper (Olaoye1995), where I looked at the limitations of the scientific method in understanding the human psyche in its totality. As a science I note that psychology is unable to reconstruct the self in all the dimensions in which people "know" it. In order to have a more adequate grasp of human functioning, the poetic method,which also develops keen observational skills, as well as heightened emotional responding, sensitivity to beauty, a proclivity to brevity and no limits to breadth or depth of subject matter,can supplement the scientific method, in gaining a fuller understanding of the human psyche. The cognitive and creative tensions that the juxtaposition of these two modes of thinking can cause in a single individual, I hypothesize, can lead to insights and integrations that foster cognitive growth . Additionally, the biological basis for this hypothesis lies in the increased systematic and frequent stimulation of both right and left brain cells.

The second function, improved coping, in reaching emotional resolutions, also has a biological basis: the explosion in neuroscientific research has provided scientists with new insights regarding the bi-directional connections between brain and behavior. The ability of poetry to create beautiful interior spaces where we enter into again and again on the breath of a wish is one of its precious capabilities. The relative ease with which we can

create these internal poetic chambers is hypothesized
to be related to the unique balance of cognitive, emotional and aesthetic factors. The power of rhyme and
rhythm ,to answer some of the deeper needs of humans is a mechanism ,by which poetry can exert an
immediate strengthening and healing experience.

Can the poetry in this volume contribute to a further
understanding and making of the modern self? maybe
even a little soul making? How might this happen?
Poetry from early to modern times, tends to fall into
two main categories: the formal finely wrought conservative poems or less formal, free flowing, fully expressive poems.The poems in this volume cover this
spectrum. Indeed many poems combine elements of
both categories. Some capture, structure and harmonize words and ideas more than others, while others
just seem to release and explode them.

What is common to all of the poems is a commitment
to express some evolving thought, allowing as many
of the conscious and unconscious impulses to propel it
and opposing tensions and energies to shape it. It is
the depth and complexity of this process rather than
the particular form that provide the compelling elements of the poems, that give them many of their essential and immediate qualities.Additionally, through
the rhythmic and rhyming properties employed, the
poems invite the reader to partake in ritual. Some
have the ritual tones associated with prayer, chant,
self-interrogation, commands and celebration. The
repetitions embodied by the poems themselves summon feelings which can bring fulfillment as do words.
In engaging this multi-faceted process, language is
used in a manner that can alter the way the reader receives it and uses it. And in turn the reader mellows,

melts or is energized, strengthened in subtle and minute ways. This is the manner in which this poetry helps with self-making and when allowed even with a little soul-making.

The seven 'Passions of' in this volume operate in this manner:they embrace different voices that give expression to the longings of the human soul and spirit.

Ars poetica (1981) written in the tradition of Kahlil-Gibran (1883-1931) examines the passions of a poet, the motives, sources of empathy, and the potency of the poetic mission. *Softly in the twilight (1981)* was inspired by a D.H. Lawrence poem and describes an inner journey guided by a poetess.

Voice patterns(1994) addresses the high-pitched anxiety that a parent may have in competing for their child's attention in a postmodern world. *To look at anyone* in contrast teaches how to use silence to gain understanding.

Join me after dusk (1984) extends an invitation to some deeper bonds of friendship.
Single one (1984) raises questions, *I want (1986)* expresses desires, the estatic notes of the latter, sharpens the formality of the former.

The ebullience of the *Ode to Spring (1967)* and the unbridled delight of *Autumn afternoon riding(1994)* and *March eve* (1997) reflect the influence of Keats and Wordsworth, poets who were a critical part of my early years.

I love to write (1995) has become an audience favorite and therefore a signature poem, its warmth and lyric flow touches hearts. In a similar, but more strident tone, *On becoming Afro-American (1994)* has stirred many to action. *I know rivers (1994)* was inspired by the Langston Hughes poem *The negro speaks of the river*. It has served to extend the flow that the potency of rivers seems to engender.

Tropical Treasures (1968) *From the Sandpiper* (1993) *Moods of Music* (1997) and *Breakthrough* (1993) touch on my Carrbbean life and heritage and come from a larger collection.

The introspection of *Thinking* (1994) dedicated to Carl G. Jung (1875-1961)and the peace and joy of *Reclined(1992)* and *For Zora Neale Hurston* (1901-1960)(1997) reflect the power of solitude and the strength that sometimes comes with maturity.

The second edition has three new poems: *Of Twin Towers,* a meditation on 9/11/01, *Knowing the Female and Knowing the Male,* a focus on the gender connection and *Rethinking Psychology,* a cognitive-emotional journey.

I hope that you will recognize in these poems the joy, power, love and hope of your own life and that in turn these passions will increase in strength, as you read and bask in their beauty and presence.

To observe students come alive in response to the poems, to see their language change as they write from their heads and their hearts, as they find and affirm themselves, has been a wonderful experience and I can only express gratitude for this privilege.

Elaine H. Olaoye
New Jersey and New York 2002

*Dedicated
to Aunt Ivy,
my daughter Temi,
my students
and the many peoples of the African diaspora
and all those who love them.*

N.B.
   "It is common knowledge that psychology is both an art and a science. The depth of human experience is best addressed by drawing from the humanities and sciences. Fowler (1998) noted the long history of the relationship between the arts and psychology, including..Division 10, "Psychology and the Arts" as a charter division of the American Psychological Association (APA) in 1945."

Nicholas Mazza, Ph.D., R.P.T. 1999
Editor, Journal of Poetry Therapy

Table of Contents

Introduction to new edition 2002................. 3
Introduction..5

On Psychology and Poetry in Self Development..6
Dedications and notation..............................14
I. Passions of the Poet....................................17
    Ars poetica..18
    Softly in the Twilight...............................20

II. Passions of a Parent...................................22
    Voice Patterns...23
    To look at anyone...................................25
    Elegy for Ivy..27

III. Passions of Friendship.......................... 30
    Join me after Dusk............................ 31
    Jaguar..33
    Knowing the female and knowing the male...34
    Exquisite one...35

IV. Passions of Love..36
    Nyack in moonlit winter..........................37
    I want..39
    Of Twin Towers....................... 41
    Angry one..42
    Single one..43
    On learning.......... 44

V Passions of the Seasons..............................45
    Ode to Spring...46
    Autumn afternoon riding.............................47
    March eve.. .49

VI. Passions of being Afro-American and Caribbean-American..................50
    I love to write..51
    On becoming Afro-American..................53
    I know rivers.......................................56
    From the sandpiper............................. 58
    Moods of music..................................59
    Breakthrough......................................61
    Tropical Treasures..............................62

VII. Passions of the soul...............................63
    Thinking... .64
    Reclined... ..65
    For Zora Neale Hurston.........................67
    Colours of Joy....................................69
    I work with you..................................70
  Slow, slow, fresh foam........................71
Rethinking Psychology.......................... 73

References..74

Appendix
1. Recipes for feeding the Soul......................75
    Introduction..75
    General Instructions 78
    Love-spiced cobblers.............................79
    Rosemaried chicken and tossed time............80
    Bitter-sweet veggies................................82
    Afro-American courage greens....................84

2. About the author......................................86
Students' responses.....................................**88**
3. Order form...89

I
Passions of a poet

Can I
am I
become as mother earth
from whose depths
the well-springs of life
gush and overflow

Ars poetica
I
(Dedicated to Kahlil Gibran)

What shall I say to him
Who has left his ball game
Or she who has left her young ones
Yearning for her breast?
What can I say
To the sons and daughters of life
That she can not already
Inscribe in their hearts?
Can I
Am I
Become as one fully laden,
Ripe with insights
That can nourish and satisfy?
II
What can I say to him
Who fears fear,
Yet who embraces fear,
And recognizes not the face of fear;
Or to she who
Endures pain,
Begets pain
And dies slowly,
Surely,
At the hands of this disguised master.

Can I,
Am I
Become as mother earth
From whose depths

New well-springs of life
Gush and overflow?

III
What can I say
To those who have all things
Yet have nothing,
For whom life remains
A darkly clouded mystery?

What can I say to those
Who are constantly charmed,
Embalmed by musical cadences
Yet
Lack the comfort they seek to find?

Can I
Am I
Become an incandescent being
With whose spirit
The rhythms of the Infinite
Might play,
And through whose voice
The dramas
And the ecstsasies of the soul
Might unfold.

1981

Softly in the twilight
I
Softly
in the twilight
A poetess is reading to me,
Taking me back
Through a passage of years,
Reawakening a crystalline memory.
'Til I see a child,
Dark-eyed
Haunted alike
By primordial ghosts of fear and truth.
'Til I see a child
Open-eyed
Encompassed equally
By the shifting shadows of darkness and light.
'Til I see a child
Wide-eyed
Attended regularly
By encircling wings of weakness and strength.
II
Softly in the darkness
A poetess is reading to me,
Taking me back
Through mists and labyrinths of time
Unlocking and opening doors of perception wide,
'Til I reach a space
Undetermined and unidentified
Where primordial fears and joys are amplified.
'Til I reach a space
Murkier than cheerless night
Where vision is blinded by darkness and by light.
'Til I reach a space
Unbounded by breadth and length
Where colossal powers

Can be ensnared by weakness and by strength.

III

In spite of myself
The bewitching mastery of words
Lures me back
To hiddenmost depths,
Where the roots of the blazing branches
Of dying autumn's
Fears, joys, dreams, and shadowed memories
Engage and surround me...
'Til as they
Slowly fall away,
A welcome warmth re-emerges.
I move forward boldly,
Feeling awakening inside,
Not only my life,
But many lives;
Now I see
Not only with my eyes
But with thousands of eyes,
Now I hear
Not only with my ears,
But with thousands of ears.
Now I speak
Not only with my voice
But with thousands of voices...
I had touched
An untold depth of life,
I had uncovered
An old kinship of lives,
Lives whose struggles
Are subject to contradictory forces as mine,
Lives that have withstood
And will withstand
The many tempests of time.

II
Passions of a parent

My tone
my cry
my voice rises
to you, it sounds like a screaming siren
responding to false alarms

Voice patterns

(For fellow postmodern parents)

At times it seems as if
I have never learned
How to bring forth each word
Each syllable to you
With perfect accent
Without anxiety or pain
In tones as smooth
As marble and sounds
As mellifluous, as fluent
As effortless, as the rhythmic flow
Of oceanward waves.

II
My tone
My cry
My voice rises,
Plaintive decibels fill the house
And pluck my heart.
They call out to the ether
They invite the witness of denizens of the farthest
galaxies.
They plead the power of penetration.
They pray for the miracle of communication.
They hope to rise above, beyond or beside,
To get through, to get past,or alongside
Millions of seductive sound bites,
Thousands of TV voices
Exhausting materialistic vices
The ever-multiplying dead-end scientifically sanc-
tioned cycles.

III
My tone
My cry
My voice rises

To you, it sounds like a screaming siren
Responding to false alarms.
Uncontrolled emotions over-reacting, over-responding
To ancient anxieties.
Over-protecting, over-anticipating the unknown
consequences
The unfamiliar patterns
Of complex options created by postmodern
Urban-suburban adolescent parental responsibilities.

IV
I have learned
How to bring forth each word
Each syllable
With perfect accent
'Without anxiety and pain
In tones as smooth as marble
And sounds as mellifluous, as fluent,
As effortless as the rhythmic flow
Of oceanward waves
My tone
My voice
Is calm and clear
As it explores, as it negotiates
The academic probabilities,
The poetic possibilities,
The emotionally distant realities.

1994

To Look at Anyone

(Respectfully dedicated to human beings everywhere)

t

To look at anyone
If you would know that one
You must look long,
You must enter into
The millions of minute silences that pattern
Their words,
Their acts,
Their moods,
Their seasons,
Their cycles.
The trillions of eloquent silences
That intertwine their words, acts, moods, seasons and cycles.
The rich background of soft silences
Waiting to be heard.

To look at any people
If you would know those people,
You must look long,
You must enter into
The trillions of coded silences that embed
Their language,
Their actions,
Their trends,
Their periods,
Their cycles.
The billions of trillions of incandescent silences
That interweave their language, actions, trends
periods and cycles.

The rich background of potent silences
So often unheard.

To look at Americans,
If you would know them
You must look long.
You must enter into
The trillions of secret silences that encode
Our speech,
Our behavior
Our moods,
Our epochs,
Our cycles.
The billions of trillions of censored silences
That interlock our communications, behavior-
moods, epochs and cycles.
The rich background of unspoken silences
Sometimes insist on being heard.

To look at African-Americans
If you would know them
You must look long
You must enter into
The trillions of silenced silences that enshroud
Our speech,
Our movements,
Our moods,
Our eras,
Our cycles.
The billions of trillions of pained silences
That interwind our speech, our movements, our
moods, our eras, our cycles.
The rich background of effluent silences
That will not be unheard.

Elegy for Ivy
I
(Dedicated to Aunt Ivy)

Mortal woman, magnificent mother
we honour your selflessness, your strength
your dedication to those around you and to those in
need
to sisters and brothers
to husband and in-laws, to nephews and nieces, to
sons and daughters, to neighbours
near and neighbours far to grandnieces and
nephews to granddaughters and sons
to strangers here and friends afar.
Behold her face
look into her eyes
when she wakes
the sun perforce must rise
Lift up your head!
behold determination stronger than steel
that willed a body to function fully
a compromised heart to beat
long after professional predictions
.acknowledged this to be a superhuman feat.

Courageous woman, ever-caring mother
we honour you as you lay to rest
as your spirit takes flight to join the
ever-blest
as you active, spontaneous, kind, ever-concerned to
the end
have created images and memories that will forever
send

energy,love, strength back to earth
through those you have blessed with your spirit, your
determination, your
commitment to an extended family now
internationally networked.

Blessed woman, beloved mother
we love you as words can never tell
even though as a family we've never learned to
express these feelings very well
we will always treasure the myriad gifts that were
yours to share
that has lead us to professions and roles beyond what
some of us might have dared
That nurtured and strengthened us that
anchored us in the values of this tropical clime
that created a sense of home that no other country can
outshine.

II
The playful waves receed but leave shells and other
treasures on the sand
a tropical sun goes down but much warmth still
embraces this island
the music of a steelband stops yet its notes echo a
lilting refrain
for every life that ends something special can remain.

III

Death makes everything more valuable
Death makes everyone more precious

Death's a time for new beginnings
Death's a pause in the pulse of human life
Death's a completion of personal accomplishments
a gift, a hope for less pain and strife.
Death's a time for deeper reflections
Death's a time for reawakening recollections
Death's a time for coming together
A time to renew our commitments to care for each other.

IV

Death's a page in vast nature's notebook
Death's a mystery though an intimate part of life
Death can be delayed but never completely
Death must fill us with love and gratitude for life.

Death transcends human understanding
Much as life signals new, uncharted beginnings
Death points always to the presence of the unknown
the abiding presence of dimensions of life not fully known

Death makes everything more valuable
Death makes everyone more precious.

III
Passions of friendship

Come ride with me
and release all cares
to winds that blow and whisper
the air will ne'er be clean nor crisper
Life's sweet!
Come, take flight and kiss her!

Join me After Dusk

I

When the sun rises, join me after dusk;
When your eyes greet the ever-widening lids of dawn,
Join me as they languish and close,
As the earth sinks into deep repose;
For dark and sweet
Are the gifts of life,
And each dawn offers a brilliant sky...
Listen as the earth sings its praises,
Watch as each season and the wind changes.
Feel the rhythm and pulse of time,
So we can cultivate,
Ah, taste
Your fruits and mine.

II

When the sun rises, join me after dusk,
When joyfully the crimson-petalled Hibiscus unfolds
To greet the morn,
Join me as its calyx closes,
As its beauty fades and decomposes;
For fragile and fleeting
Are the gifts of life,
And each moment offers us a cloistered clue...
When we can renew our thrust, our quest
For an illumined life,
When we catch a glimpse of the meaning
Of personal strife;
When we can discover sequestered secrets locked
In the labyrinths of time,
And so occasion and increase
A vital process
That may never cease.

III

When the sun rises, join me after dusk,
When the night-blooming blossoms of Cereus droop
and wane
In the blazing light of day,
Join me as its essence gradually night encloses,
As this fragrant efflorescent bud, its exotic beauty
discloses;
For rich and ripe
Are the gifts of life
And each terrestrial eve offers us a womb sublime...
Where we rediscover our roots, our powers and the
magic of time,
Where we recreate our thoughts, our lives our
dreams,
Where we meander through the infinite wealth of
humankind,
Regaining the joy, the essence of our authentic kind,
Tasting the fruit,
The nectar,
From our branch of the cosmic vine.

1984

Jaguar

(For Leo J)

Come ride with me
and let the breezes tease
the curly lengths of your dark hair
and stroke and playfully caress
your melanin-brown cheeks and honeyed eyes.

Come ride with me
and let the billion happy leaves
their playful carefree spirit share
and tease your glowing eyes and soften the glare
and make the countryside graceful and fair.

Come ride with me
indeed my heart with joy is beating
transported by the freedom that before us lies
and the melliflous sounds that effortlessly fly
and die when driving in flowing feline motion.

Come ride with me
and release all cares
to the winds that blow and whisper
the air will ne'er be clean nor crisper
Life's sweet, come! take flight and kiss her!

1996

Knowing the Male and Knowing the Female

Knowing the female
And
Knowing the male
One becomes
Co-creator once more
Of the secret patterns of eternity
Knowing the male
And
Knowing the female
Is to value
Fullness and void
Sound and silence
Form and space.
Knowing the female
And
Knowing the male
Is to value
Non-action and action
Light and dark
Intuition and law.
Knowing the male
And
Knowing the female
Is to value
The mutual necessity
Of pulse and pause in vibration
The mutual generativity
Of positive and negative poles in electricity
Knowing the female
And
Knowing the male
Is to experience
The mutual inseparability
Of Heaven and Earth.

Why confuse all this
With good and bad?

Exquisite One

(For Ellen F)

Just as in the tropical isles
Satin-petalled lilies
Stand matchless
Newborn
Regal resplendent
Delicate and warm,
So is your presence.

Just as in spring
Fresh water gushes forth
With wide flashes of foam
So is your smile
Exquisite one.
And as rivulets and streams
Sparkle and cascade
Playfully down to sea
Such is the lucid beauty
Of your speech and laughter.

Yet as you grace the earth
With your petal weight
Lightning bolts of passion emanate
And spiritual light and joy radiate
From your eternal core.
With what strength, beauty, clarity and joy
You open the petals of your life
Blossoming lily of the world.

1986

IV
Passions of love

With you
I want
to quiver and quiver and quiver
with the delight of millions of trillions
of new-born rustling leaves

Nyack in moonlit winter

(Dedicated to Pablo Neruda)

My love
We have found each other
Thirsty
And we hesitate to drink at
Each other's fount
All the water and the wine
We were destined to store
For each other.
My love
We have found each other
Hungry
And we hesitate to eat at
Each other's table
The bread , the fruit
We have prepared for each other.

II

I slept with you
All night long
While the Hudson outside lay fair,
Aglow in the moonlight;
While the gently billowing waves
Splashed playfully against the pebbled shoreline below.
On waking, in the midst of silent shadows
And tremulous cadences of the wind in the evergreens
I was protected by your embrace,
Your arms encircled me,
Neither night nor sleep
Had separated us.

III

I slept with you all night long
While the snow changed
The fir trees and bare branches in the garden
Into a sparkling bridal cathedral.
On waking,
Your mouth came from your dreams
From the depths of your life
And you gave me a taste of earth,
Of struggles, of daring , of determining.
I received your kiss
Purified by the blue and golden light of dawn
As it broke over the moving tide of the Hudson,
A kiss moistened by a morning glow of faith
And destined to echo through the day
With the timeless secrets of love.

1987

I want

I

I want
To re-consummate the joys
The pleasures
The beauty
Of spring
In your arms.

I want
To begin with the
Quiet beauty of the trilliums
And the blue and white and yellow violets
That in early spring carpet the woodland floors.
I want
To be filled
With the regal splendour
Of sun-kissed tulips,
And the blithesome playfulness
Of sun-drenched daffodils.
With you
I want
To quiver and quiver and quiver
With the delight of millions of trillions
Of new-born rustling leaves.

II

With you
I want
To express the crystalline clarity
Of melting, crackling ice and snow.
And chuckle , laugh and flow
With the replenished vigour
And the ever-fluid grace
Of hundreds of rivulets

Breaking forth and running free.
With you
I want
To quietly expand
And swell
And burst with
The passionate blaze of azaleas.

III

I want
To climb the mountainsides
And breathe the freshest air
And rise resplendent
With spring triumphant
And see winter
Liquid and repentant.
I want
To reconsummate spring
In you
Until the perennial winters
Of doubt and depression
Yield to the inexorable
And unalterable
Fountainhead of ever-regenerating spring.
I want
To reconsummate spring
In you
Until
My love becomes like
The seeds and bulbs and buds of spring,
And grow and open
With infinite grace and beauty
Seeking and kissing life
Until we are enjoined, entwined
In an eternally fertile and fragrant flowering.

1985

Of Twin Towers

Millions of
Eyelids in
New York
Blink, tear
As hate's
Venom
Spreads its
Destructive
Wings and
Devours the
Towers
Death and
Destruction
Pour down
From the air.
The innocent
Air. Travelers
The innocent
Forced kami-
kaze accom-
plices, create
A hell hotter
Than Dante's
Inferno in
Seconds
Cremating
Thousands
Of innocents
Vaporizing
Twin steel
Skyscrapers
Into a cloud
Of unbelievable
Ash. Mankind
Achieves all its
Technological
Dreams, but
Never peace.
Technologically
Efficient the
Towers and
Bodies burn
At 2000 degrees

As the sun
Bright unmoved
Continues to
Shine over New
York, the ashes
Of the innocent
Rise to greet
The morning
Rays. When
They vanish
With eventide
Spirals of incense
From my soul
Will ascend on
Sorrowful wings
To bless them.
But destruction has
Been in men's
Hearts for a long
While. And some
Times at the last
Gasp comes peace
And light to the
Soul...and what
Comes to us
Who are left
Through the
Shock, the pain
The grief, the
Anger, the
Vengeance, the
Smouldering fires
The smoke, the
Ash, the remains
Of bodies, the
Vigilance of the
Faithful? The
Gentle inclination
To contemplate anew
The twin powers of
Life and Death
The twin towers
Of love and hate

Angry one
I
This is our moment of madness,
Oh, angry one,
When we engage each other
As relentlessly as the waves
That beat upon the seashore
When we inflame each other
As passionately as the raging
Seaspray on the gutted rocks.
II
This is our moment of wretchedness
Oh, angry one,
When wronged and wounded
We weep blinded by piteous claims;
When galled and grieved
We roar, deaf to each other's utterances
III
This is our moment of danger
Oh, angry one,
When in us wars, weapons
And wounds open and accumulate,
When in us
The mad coupling of passion and fury
Clash and merge.
IV
This is our moment of surrender
Oh, angry one,
When spent and weary
We signal involuntary cessation,
When softened and sober
We embrace
Glad that we are sane again.
1981

Single one

Single one
each celestial star is destined to journey far
to traverse eons of time in place,
past planetal orbs with consummate grace,
so are we destined
each to journey through inner space
piercing mysteries like birth and death
transcending mankind's dependence on a single breath.
Single one
just as each celestial star
though destined to journey far
is surrounded by many billlion stars
each meteor-like in speed and grain, moving
in galaxies of vast and several planes,
dauntlessly each other pass;
so we chivalrous or bold
do each our unique perspectives hold
moving always as seems we must
lest, indeed we blunt out thrust.
Single one
Indeed each celestial star
is destined to journey far
but, ah, not always each alone.
Some do, in time, in space, their doubles find
And in playful apposition each other bind
Can we, will we,
in this space, for a single moment in time
experience the powerful forces which join
moon to Earth and Earth to sun
Or that which joins protons and neutrons
One to one?
Can we, will we
In equilibrium find each other's center,
In this space, in this time?

On Learning

*For all my Psychology students at
Brookdale Community College and John Jay College of Criminal
Justice
Yes! There is no joy in living, if there is no joy in learning!*

I love the delicate dawning
Of fresh thoughts scarcely spawning
The first fledgling forms
Or notions
Of feelings, ideas
Yearnings
Shy diffident
Unyielding
To usual manipulation,
Thoughts which in keen
And cloistered sequestration
With tireless time
And gentle cultivation
Weaves from doubt
And elusive contradictions
Profound and poignant
Integrations.

1986

V
Passions of the seasons

Season of joyful splendour and
rejuvenation
welcome re-creation are you,
Oh, Spring
with what delight and eager anticipation
do we await your longed-for coming
you seem to shed an effulgent light
on simply everything in sight
Oh, loveliest season, can you hear
our cry to you to stay all year?

Ode to Spring

(Dedicated to John Keats)

I

Season of joyful splendour and rejuvenation
welcome re-creation are you , oh Spring
with what delight and eager anticipation
do we await your longed-for coming
you seem to shed an effulgent light
on simply everything in sight
oh, loveliest season can you hear
our cry to you to stay all year?

II

With such gentle motion you descend
with such calm and subtle equipose
yet so blithesome and efflorescent
full of the dreams that each heart holds
all of your lovers rejoice and sing
awake! be happy! for here comes Spring
and mankind seem to join the refrain
celebrating, applauding that you're here again.

III

You dress nature in her very best
the streams and rivulets babble happily once more
the longing earth again is blest
with graceful flowers and herbage all o'er
the birds sing out their sweetest songs
they saved for you all winter long
you awaken the world to such an ethereal sight
Oh, Spring you are an eternal delight!.

1967

Autumn Afternoon Riding

(For Art W)

I

A western autumn sun is
a jeweled light
transforming leaves
to burnished golds
flaming reds
incandescent glows.
to a blushing show
of gushing rows of branched blossoms
flanked, ranked
reaching upwards, outwards
giving, changing
row after row
to brown and golden yellows
soon falling in cascading showers
carpeting still-green grassy bowers.

II

A western autumn sun is
a precious light
lasting only a few fleeting hours
before twilight
stealthily creeps and o'er it towers
lasting only a few fast-fading weeks
when leaves colour and invariably seek
a glorious destiny, a triumphant fall
a date with death
and splendid spectacles for all.

III

A western autumn sun is
a wondrous light
creating a scintillating world for human sight
amber-lit woodlands
carpeted in burnished gold
the glow of blushing valleys
with jeweled majesty after majesty to behold
glowing, flaming branches set against
azure and sapphire skies
gracing leave-splashed grasslands
of rolling hills and plains
creating unending splendours again and again
live bouquets of enormous scale
shimmering, glimmering with all their might
celebrating, vibrating
throwing kisses to the sky
and bidding us all a fond goodbye.

1994

March Eve
(For Steve P)

This March evenmg
is the most beautiful of the year
filled with camelot castles, cathedrals
and chandeliers
snow-kissed
and majestically dressed evergreens
tall
finely sculpted leaf-fleeced deciduous trees...
Oh! the awesome grandeur
of these woodland scenes
snowlight falling, twinkling
setting aglow this winter eve
with mystery, moisture, beauty and innocence
what a wondrous magnificence!
My winter evening grows intricate
and soooo immense
snowbuds blossom
as well as frosty trims on gates and fence
the enveloping darkness enfolds me
in a pregant moment with ease
as I espy
newly decked displays of gaily-branched
white dogwoods
and once apple-blossomed trees...
I pause
I ponder
I savour the joy...
from whence
to hence
this precious gift
these sacred moments
these splendid memories forming of the year.
1997

VI
Passions of being Afro-American and Caribbean-American

I love to write
I want to write
of the unheralded triumphs of my people
of the myriad scientific inventions
of sweet melodies and glorious
arrangements of musicians
of billions of unforgettable
unerasable, still traceable contributions
maintaining this nation.

I Love to Write

(Dedicated to Oprah Winfrey)

I

I love to write
I want to write
The unspoken words of my people
The sacred words
The words of faith
The word of hope
The words ignored by history.

I love to write
I want to write
Of the undying love of my people
Their love of Life
Their joy in Life
Their intimacy with Life
So often omitted from their story.

II

I love to write
I want to write
Of the incandescent beauty given to my people
Of the ageless grace
Of agile energies defying time and space
Of the youthful glowing face
Exfoliated by unending seasons
of adversity.

I love to write
I want to write
Of the infinite patience required of my people
For whom so often the world it seems
Is a country of ever-elusive dreams
For limited inheritable resources are
monopolized by the majority.

III
I love to write
I want to write
Of the quiet power nurtured in my people
The discipline of enduring pain
Of billions of decisions
To forgive, to forego again and again
Cruel insults that emotionally cripple and maim.

I love to write
I want to write
Of the unheralded triumphs of my people
Of myriad scientific inventions
Of sweet melodies and glorious arrangements of
musicians
Of billions of unforgettable
Unerasable, still traceable contributions
maintaining this nation.

1994

On Becoming an Afro-American

(Dedicated to Martin Luther King Jr.)

I

Breakout
Of the suffocating shell
Of Eurocentric racism
A temporary prison
Built of power
Greed and materialism.
Breakfree
Of centuries of indoctrination
And attempts at annihilation
Coupled with physical and mental persecution.
Breakout
Of polarized tensions of Democrats and Republicans
Of discomfort created by conservative and liberal
condescension,
Of the disappointment borne of impotent and
lacklustre legislation.

II

Breakfree
Of shame, of doubt, of financial limitation
Low self-esteem, exclusion and so-called
Cultural deprivation
And dream
And hope
And see
The coming of a new humanity.
And mould
And build
And bring
A new being to birth
From these centuries of suffering.

III

Make
Each tear
Each wound
Each life
Be an unforgettable offering
In this painful and victorious strife.
No innocent life was taken in vain.
And time and patience are healing the links
Not only in the broken African chain
But providing the strength by which
Equal status as Americans will be claimed and
sustained.

IV

Breakout !
Breakfree !
African-American
Explore interiority
Chart unknown territory
Past crumbling bourgeoisie and aristocracy
Past so-called working class mediocrity,
Past decadent Puritan theology
And fading Marxist ideology
Past the crippling influences of modern technology
Past the meaningless manipulations of postmodern
society.
Let a dying civilization
Bury its dead.
You have survived
Its most sinister dread.
You are still not perceived to this society to be wed.

Take charge of the destiny
You were spared to spearhead.

V

African-American
Breakout !
Breakfree !
Leave the shackles of racism behind.
Give them back to those who aspire to make people un-
free.
Let accurate accountings of history
And their superegos
Their true judge be.

African-American
Breakout !
Breakfree !
In moments of empowering privacy
(Drug free)
With penetrating and piercing clarity
And periods of increasing frequency
Let blossom the new humanity.

1994

I Know Rivers
(Dedicated to Langston Hughes and Alexander Barton)

I

I know rivers
Timeless, majestic, deliberate
In their movement
The crushing weight and dazzling beauty
Of ice-blue glaciers.

I know rivers
I know rivers
Ever-renewing, ageless, undulating
In their translucent constancy
The fluid flowing fertile form
Of famed and ancient rivers.

My soul grows deep like a river.

II

I know rivers
I know rivers
Swift, scathing, hot, molten
Deadly, daring, destructive
In their uncharted transfixing
And uncertain paths.

I know rivers
I know rivers
Suffocating, stifling, constricting
Deadening, overwhelming
constructing graves of villages
In their tumultuous flow.

My soul grows deep like a river.

III

I know rivers
I know rivers
The flow, the tides of constant
And changing generations of humanity
Time- constructed seriality
Imposed upon ongoing multidimensionality.

I know rivers
I know rivers
Dominating torrents
Confluences of cultural pluralities
Conceptual currents and contradictory eddies
And floods of blood and tears.

I know rivers
I know rivers
Infinite, flowing
Ever-changing complexities
Of human and non-human realities.

I know rivers.

My soul grows deep like a river.

1994

From the Sandpiper

(For Dawn)

The trade winds blew and oceanward made,
The billowing waves crashed, splashed and drifted
Thousands of thoughts surfaced , from inner depth
displayed
And in fluid sequence to morning light was lifted
Seagulls soared upwards, outwards, darting diving
against the vast expanse of sky
Their graceful flight compelling appreciation
for the motioned beauty of these feathered creatures
as they fly.
Thousands more thoughts to moving, flowing ,cresting
waves are released
Follow, follow follow their undulating journey that
doesn't seem to cease
The fluid grace of the seaward motions, the playful
breaking of white foam,
Rising and falling, rising and falling, again and again.
Motioned thoughts from billions of hearts radiating
Outward, upward, backward, forward, downward
through the vast expanses of time and space
Charting their invisible trajectories, their unseen
flights to trillions of different places.
More constant than the wafting waves traveling out or
coming in from the sea
Swifter far, than the seagull's arching flight
is the movement of the human plea.

Crosbies, Antigua
1993

Moods of Music

(Dedicated to Maurice and Marlon)
Crosbies, Antigua

There's always music
the perpetual rhythm, flow of things
of love, of work, of longing
of struggle, of heartache, of joy,
of "yes",
of limitation, of celebration
of meditation, of deliberation
There's always music
tearing off the masks
of meaninglessness
and revealing
the emotional face of time.
There's always music,
the motion of
millions of waves, energies coming in
aquamarine races
splashing drifting
frothing rhythmically
as they skip and skim
from a distant horizon to the playful ripples of the
bay.
There's always music
frequently chords and notes of a grand piano
but sometimes clarinet, flute,recorder
original arrangements, more often improvisations
on Bach, Chopin, Ellington,Purcell,Gershwin
Rutter, follow each other in any order
on any day regardless of mood

or myriad matters.
There's always music
piano and recorder rehearsals,
duets, solos, choruses
earnest expressions , hallowing places
honouring occasions, santifying spaces,
creating bonding experiences.
There's always music
on M-TV, on latest CDs
in surround sound:
pass-the-time music
assist-the-computer music
drown-out-the feelings music
dream-of-a-brighter-day music
love-me-again music
heal-the-earth music
bring-back-those-memories music
lets-get-to-work music
take-me-away music
lets-go-to-sleep music.
There's always music
in these cathedraled-cielinged spaces
rising upward, outward flowing through
sky-scaped paned windows
releasing notes that float
over frolicking and shimmering bays
and with seagulls and pelicans
carry melodies and messages
to places and loved ones far away.

Crosbies, Antigua
1997

Breakthrough

*(Dedicated to Claude McKay and all my
Medgar Evers students 1986 to present)*

Breakthrough the limiting walls
Of seductive materialism
Of fragile privilege;
Sift through the ruins
Of cultural heritages
Of moral wreckages;
Mix the mortar
Of the new era of personhood
From the dust of these idols and traditions.

Assume all possible assumptions,
Break the shell of sterile conventions
Build bonds with Africans, Latinos, Asians,
Insects, animals, rain forests, Earth's vegetation,
Bonds of mutual respect and cooperation
And forsake the futility, the sterility
of overt and covert
desires
for domination.

1993

Tropical Treasures

I lay on Central Park's summer grass
Reliving encounters with Antigua in the past:
The ever-changing azures of the sea
Glistening with peaks sparkling brilliantly
Delicously cool under the noonday's sun
I met the challenging, concave surf with a run.
Or lying lazily, half-turned to the side
Watching the playful languid lapping tide
Creeping, ever-widening lacy-edged on the sand
Reaching up to touch the tips of my hand.

And then I thought of the dewy morns
When I rose very early just about dawn
And felt the cool crystal deliciousness
That comes only with the morning freshness.
The twittering robins in their nest
The hush that comes when people are at rest;
The jeweled flowers awakening with smiles
Clothed in rich tropic colours barely espied
Blues, crimsons and golds among hardy leaf greens
In the softened splendour of an auroral scene.

And then I remembered the succulent fruit
Rich, golden and ripe, overflowing with juice
Mangoes and plums, sugar apples and grapes
Ambrosia for gods, any appetite they'd sate
Free for the plucking, as many as you please
Filling overgrown groves with apparent ease
The memory I thought was really a treasure
Storing so vividly these moments of pleasure;
So wherever I go, however long I roam
I will always have my island home.

1968

VII
Passions of the Soul

Return, fair hope
resume thy seat
and to each waiting soul impart
the gladsome tidings of thy heart.

Return! fair hope
with mien so soft
yet so powerful and so clear
that all behold thy immortality here!

Thinking
(Dedicated to Carl G. Jung)

I

Much of thinking
Is mere dreamwork
Wish fulfillment
A potent personal power
By which we multiply distinctions
And discover intricate causal and correlational functions
By which we develop individual trajectories
And carve out the forms of daily and final destinies.

II

Much of thinking
Is less than dreamwork
Non-fulfillment
A potent frustrating power
By which we multiply confusions
And pursue ancient ideas already doomed to extinction
A power by which we reinforce our isolation and our prejudices
And justify our greed and pursuit of endless indulgences.

III

Much of thinking
Is more than dreamwork
Personal fulfillment
A transcendent suprapersonal power
By which we multiply illuminations
And shatter millions of seductive and fearful illusions.
By which we open and reopen creative spaces
And turn on light in once dark and unintelligible places.
Where ever-changing permutations and combinations bring
Continued insights that reality is an infinite expression of infinitely moving things.

1994

Reclined

(For Nathaniel O)

I

On a sun-warmed deck in early noon
A lingering note of summer,
A soothing balm
A gentle kiss
Hugs
Unlike those from a lover
Invite the inklings, the possibility,
The presence of still another.

II

Reclined
On a leaf-littered autumn afternoon,
Embraced by a symphony of magnificent colour:
Bouquets of golden lightened trees
Trumpeting tunes received by a deep blue ether,
Blushing red-orange trees
Others dark-exotic, burgundy-leaved
Anchored all by black-barked sheaves,
Awesome, tall and gracefully seized.

III

Reclined
On a blustery October noon
Cascading showers of autumn-coloured leaves descend,
Thousands of air-borne missives portend...
Azure-blue skies, fathomless, boundless in their clarity
Create wonder, the unceasing musings about eternity,
And zephyrs waft, rustle, tickle and sway
Thoughts and feelings of earthly exuberance
In this theatre of natural magnificence.

IV
Reclined
On a mellow receptive harvest noon
I feel your warmth and wealth and generous open hand
The abundant gifts, the endless flow
Of physical delight for human enjoyment planned.
Can we be so unmindful and not thank you for these gifts
Nor trust that you who made us and this wondrous abode
Might have the power to help us seek
And find the secrets of creative bliss?

1993/ 1994

For Zora Neale Hurston

Drunk with the scent of Casablanca lilies
baskets of goodbyes   and
baskets of kisses
twinkling twilight blossoming in beauty as it fades
a russet sunset wide as the horizon's rim
awakening memories even as they fly
they skim   they drift along
conscious and subconscious shores

transformations of the mind
temporal and spatial flux
invisible   polyvocal
polydramatic   autopoetic
inscribing on emotional
sensual   lyric flesh

the feeling of colour
the colour of feeling

the chaos of thought
the thought of chaos

the illusion of nothingness
the nothingness of illusion

the yearning for union
the union of yearning

the silence of words
the words of silence

the passion of tenderness
the tenderness of passion

the restlessness of stillness
the stillness of restlessness

like tendrils in the night
the mind seeks solace
in surging contradictions
that lead ever
stray further
into elemental   not definable forms
eluding the magic of language
eternally in flight
as a wave
poised somewhere between dream
and silence   taking flight from joy
or anguish to oblivion
a tremulous tune of fugitive sounds
cresting the ether   in time and timelessly
when spent
a sad happiness envelops me
and my soul folds like nocturnal flower.

1997

Colours of Joy
Let all the colours
sounds   of   joy
burst   swell
into life-giving poetic song
painting the beauty of
not desiring
not possessing   not wanting
that which o'er burdens
with endless debt
self-destroying habits
visions of famine lack death
Let all the colours
sounds of joy
burst   swell
into ever-rising poetic song
titillating the senses
embracing   in the bondage
of natural pleasures
all day   all night   long
til with taste   touch
sight   hearing   smell
surfeited on nature's bounty
soothed   healed   with this much
what first appears   as   illusions
slowly   turn   into mind-expanding illuminations
what first begins as desires
slowly   develop   into fiber optic cables of love
transforming words   notes   and silences
echoing throughout the skies in many-coloured tones
falling tear-drops   spiraling hopes
and clouded smiles
Wondrous dramas   ever near
initially perceived by eye and ear

*(Dedicated to Fellow Minority Psychologists
upon receipt of the Ph.D. by Y. Thorne)*

I work with you

I work with you for the dawn
Of coming psychological sophistication
When skills will focus
More on human discipline and compassion
And less on
Statistical pretensions and manipulations.

I work with you for the dawn
Of coming psychological sophistication
When skills will be shared adequately
With members of all ethnic groups of our nation
And concentrated less
On the self-defeating goals
Of proving ethnic inferiority
And engaging in or ignoring
Excessive material acquisition.

I welcome with you the dawn
Of current psychological sophistication
Where women are making
Larger critical contributions
To the understanding and development
Of ego individuation
And distinctions between
And characteristics of
Pathological and existential emotions.

1995

Slow, slow

I

Slow, slow
Fresh foam
Keep time with my encroaching fears.
Slow, slow,
Salt foam
Make visible my useless tears.
Slower,
still slower yet,
List to the heavy thought the heart bears,
The incessant contradictions
In which modern man is ensnared.

II

Weapons multiply in horror before the unbelieving brain;
Violence and more violence follow in their train.
Computers, technology promising new freedoms to each job and profession
Instead releases us
Into a new series of endless obsessions.
Satellites giving us wider visions of the skies
Allow nations to become better spies
And catches us all in multidimensional white lies.
Television the best technology for edification and information
Uses symbols of affluence to breed poverty not from hardship
But through unrealistic expectations.
Statistics crunch millions of numbers,
Conclusions at a glance,
While numbing our minds
And multiplying much organized ignorance.

III
Slow, slow,
Fresh foam
Keep time with changing years.

Slow, slow
Salt foam
Make visible yet unseen ideas.

Slower
Still slower yet,
List to the new sounds an enlightened heart hears
As it plummets new depths
And with flights of imagination,
soars!

1993

RETHINKING PSYCHOLOGY

For over twenty-five years
Gathering the fragments of an ancient
An broken dream
The pieces
Lisping a language
Elusive ... Dance
Dazzling the mind
Weaving loops of excitement
Anticpation and trepidation
Loops of wonder
Loops of longing
Loops of openings
Laced with flashes of boldness
And bolts of energy.
For twenty-five years
Gathering the fragments
Of a modern and scientific logic
The pieces
Distilling a discpline
But slipping on a steep
Epistemological slope
Splinter
Splitting into still smaller
Snippets of knowledge
Stitching a fabric of the psyche
With statistical, biological
And experimental threads
Emotionless
The structures of modern psychology emerge.
Looking at the next twenty-five years
Gathering fragments
Of a radiant, of a powerful vision
The pieces
Whispering transcendent tales
Sparkle and play along new ways
Rejecting Newtonian mechanical moulds
Leaping forward, experiencing new images of relativity
Leaping beyond outdated paradigms of reality
Leaping beyond words into new levels of awareness...

References

Abbs, Peter, "The Development of Autobiograhy in Western Culture: From Augustine to Rousseau" Thesis, University of Sussex 1986, 130; 131-132.

Fowler, R. D. The healing arts, *APA Monitor*, 29 (March), 3, 1998.

Mazza, Nicholas "Poetry Therapy: Interface of the Arts and Psychology. Boca Raton, Florida: CRC Press 1999.

Mezirow, J. Transformative Dimensions of Adult Learning. San Francisco: Jossey-Bass 1991.

Olaoye, Elaine H. ".Reconnecting with the Emotional Domain in Analyzing Research in Psychology: The Role of Informal and Poetic Writing in Psychology" Paper presented to the Second National Conference on "Writing Across the Curriculum", Charleston, South Carolina, February, 1995.

Olaoye, Elaine H. "Essential Hypertension and Anxiety, Depression and Anger" Ph.D. Dissertation, University Center/CUNY, New York, Dissertaion Abstracts, 1981

Rubin, Z. Liking and Loving: An invitation to Social Psychology. New York: Holt, Rinehart and Winston. 1973.

Stort, Anthony *Solitude: A Return to the Self.* New York: Ballantine Books, 1988, 75.

Vendler, Helen *The Music of What Happens* Cambridge, MA: Harvard University Press, 1988

Zimbardo, Philip, G., Weber, Ann L, and Johnson, Robert Lee *Psychology* 3rd Edit., Needham Heights, M: Allyn & Bacon. 2000.

Appendix

Recipes for Healing the Mind and Feeding theSoul

Imagination is more important than knowledge
                                        Einstein

INTRODUCTION
Psychology involves research and application, followed by transformation. Poetry involves immersion and agency followed by transformation. In a world as complex as ours we have to make the time to create or find what nurtures our soul. We also have to find processes that anchor us in our lives and cause us to find the wealth and health awaiting us.With the help of your imagination you are invited to use cooking and eating as metaphors to provide some of the particular nutrients your mind and soul long for and need.

SETTING
Physical space: Quiet, indoor or outdoor with or without chosen background instrumental music.
Psychological space: One of heightened imagination, increased emotional appetite and a strong desire to understand and nurture oneself.
Behavioral posture: Relaxed, seated or lotus position, or meditative walking both accompanied by deep breathing.More active rituals such as dancing, clapping, laughing and smiling release energy, permit celebration, experiences important in transformation Also using one hand to gently stroke the other helps with anchoirng positive feelings and experiences.

Appliances needed
1. An adjustable emotionally-fired oven.
2. An energy-propelled food processor.
3. An intellectually controlled refrigerator.
4. An anger-piloted stove.
5. An imagination-powered microwave oven.

Utensils
1. A resilience-coated wooden spoon.
2. An emotionally-transparent mixing bowl.
3. A patience-primed baking dish.
4. A joyfully sparkling serving dish.

Principles
The concept of the recipes comes out of the research on stress and stress management (Olaoye 1981). The specific focus from this area of research is on :

1. How our memories and perceptions help create or increase stress in our lives.

2. How we can take responsibility for responding to and working with these memories and perceptions to control and reduce stress in our lives.

We are our memories and perceptions. But they are not necessarily true nor are they immutable. This is the focus of the metaphor of cooking: Just as we can transform meats and vegetables into healthy meals, we are challenged to observe our memories and perceptions (rather than take them always as givens) and restructure them so they serve us better, so they feed us rather than feed on us. We learn how to turn them into fuel for our life, how to create eustress out of stress.

The psychological principles that can be employed to do this can be operationalized by an imaginative action of cooking, mixing, bringing together different ingredients. Juxtaposing in very short time "good" and "bad" feelings, joyous and anxious memories, alternating experiences of anger and gratitude, for example, can be powerful change agents, that can lead to new visions, energies and perspectives.

The imaginative tasks of cooking are backed by the psychological principles of classical and operant conditioning as well as those of reciprocal inihibition and opponent process theory. Without these creating a foundation for the steps in the recipes, they would have a low probability of working.

Additionally the tradition of keeping an inventory, of making a shopping list and being able to go shopping for what you need, is also an operating principle of this chosen metphor. Most of us run short of patience, energy, imagination etc and need to decide where and when do we replenish our supplies.

I have created four recipes for you. One for experiencing love in relationships, one for coping with stress, one for dealing with loss and one for dealing with racism and sexism. Try one this evening, especially if you were moved by the poems involved. or the recipe identifies something that you need to work on.

Whatever you do relax, observe yourself, chuckle and have fun. Honour and celebrate yourself. Then , when so inclined, try a recipe with a spouse, friend or co-worker. Tell me if it works for you, by dropping me a line at the address on the order form.

General Instructions

- Take ingredients out of your mental cabinet and also observe what is missing.
- Make arrangements to acquire missing ingredients from a "supermarket".
- Inspect each of the ingredients and note the feelings they generate.
- Identify those with the strongest joyous feelings
- Identify those with the strongest anxious feelings.
- Mix gently ingredients with the strongest 'good' or joyous feelings with those with the strongest 'bad' or anxious feelings together.
- Always have on hand gallons of patience, commitment, imagination and love.
- When mixing opposite feelings be prepared to add slowly gallons of the above.
- You must also shop regularly for gallons of energy and initiative as well as patience, commitment, love and imagination.
- Most recipes will require that you stir in gallons of the above from time to time.
- You will have to use your emotional appetite as well as knowledge, as a guide in creating a nutritious and satisfying meal for you.
- You will have to sample your creation, chew on it, digest a little of it, test it, before it may be right for you.
- When it hits the emotional spot note the characteristics and serve yourself generous helpings garnished with humour and joy. You have to feed yourself daily until there is some tangible degree of transformation. This can take months!
- *Bon appetit!*

Recipes

(Amounts of ingredients will vary with individuals)

1. Love Spiced Cobblers

3 pureed peaches
3 wks work-related intimacy deprivation
6 hrs of supervisor/peer aggravation
6 evenings of chores and conflict mediation
3 hrs of media-mediated sensual stimulation
5 yrs of conjugal commitment
6 years of love (chilled)
8 yrs of grace (frozen)
7 yrs of affection (ice packed)
   Nyack in Moonlit Winter............................ 37
   I Want...39

1. Place all ingredients in full view.

2. Put love, grace and affection in your imagination powered microwave to defrost and revive them.

3. Mix together years of commitment and love with weeks of deprivation and aggravation while reading *Nyack in Moonlit Winter,* (Part I.)

4. As you read and reread Part I, knead all the ingredients in #3 into a dough, breathing deeply and letting the dough massage your hands, until feeling more comforted you are ready to place the dough into patience-primed baking dishes.

5. Place pureed peaches, warm love, affection and grace in an emotionally transparent mixing bowl

and stir sensuously while reading *I Want* (Part I).

6. Breathing deeply, taste your filling to see that is emotionally spiced with as much love, grace and affection as you need while reading *I Want* (Part II).

7. Arrange these love spiced peaches on the pastry dough of commitment and bake in an emotionally-adjusted oven, while reading *Nyack in Moonlit Winter* (Parts II and III).

8. Serve warm in joyfully sparkling serving dish. Savour, relish and eat until satisfied , while reading *I Want* (Part III).

9. Prepare, serve and eat languorously twice a day for 3 months or until recalling a phrase brings back. these images and feeling wherever and whenever you have a need to be in touch with them.

2. Rosemaried Chicken and Tossed Time

Rosemary
3 mths overload and impatience.
3 mths of running (like a chicken without a head).
2 mths of punitive internalized deadlines
5 years of patience(frozen)
5 years of commitment
5 years of grace (frozen)
Thinking 64
Colors of Joy.................................69
Softly in the Twilight............................. 20
Infinite time

1. Place all ingredients in full view

2. Trim and toss away impatience and cut up overload in to small pieces and store some in the intellectually-controlled refrigerator by reading *Thinking* Part II.

3. Place patience and grace in the imagination-powered microwave to defrost them.

4. Marinate chicken with patience and commitment by reading *Softly in the Twilight* (Part I). Add some new age music to this marinade if desired. Breathe deeply.

5. Place chopped overload, internalized deadlines, grace and rosemary in emotionally tranparent mixing bowl, tossing them rhythmically, while reading *Softly in the Twilight* (Part II). Forget about time.

6. When filled with relaxed and mellow memories, smother chicken with tossed deadlines, rosemarie etc, and bake in oven for infinite time while reading *Softly in the Twilight* (Part III).

7. Serve with a dash of abandon and more tossed time, in a joyfully sparkling serving dish by reading *Colors of Joy*.

8. Prepare, serve and eat with deliberate abandon twice daily for at least 3 months or until recalling a particular phrase brings back feelings of relaxation and control where and whenever you need them.

3. Bitter-Sweet Veggies

Sweet potatoes   Varieties of lettuce
2 wks loneliness   10yrs strength
2 wks loss of loved one or job   10yrs love
2 wks low energy   10yrs grace
2 wks disinterest in pleasure 10yrs patience
10yrs gratitude
Ars Poetica...18
Elegy for Ivy 27
Reclined..65
Sacred music if desired

1. Relax create a quiet space and place all ingredients gently on a kitchen counter.

2. Mix reassuring chord of chosen music with your loss, loneliness and low energy until energies begin to rise by reading Elergy for Ivy Part I, Verses II and III.

3. Wash sweet potatoes in memories of love then let them bake seasoned with patience and strength by reading *Ars Poetica* (Part II).

4. Peel and discard skins by reading *Elegy for Ivy* (Part II)..

5. Slowly begin to prepare a glaze by folding gently your loss into generous honeyed-measures of love and grace. Do this by alternating memories of loss with memories

6. Complete the glaze by reading *Elegy for Ivy* (Part III), adding more love, grace and gratitude.

7. Pick up peeled potatoes by rereading *Elegy for Ivy* (Part II).

8. Place in a dish, cover with glaze and bake in a warm emotional oven by reading *Elegy for Ivy* (Part IV). Bake until comfortable and firm. Breathe deeply.

9. Serve warm on a bed of lettuce with bitter herbs (pain of loss). by reading *Reclined* Part I.

10. Partake slowly and thoughtfully with ritual, until strengthened and comforted by reading *Reclined*, Part IV.

Prepare, serve, savour and eat twice daily for at least 3 months or until recalling a phrase can bring you comfort and resolve wherever and whenever you need them.

4. Afro-American Courage Greens

2 lbs collard and other greens
10 yrs racism and sexism
10 yrs economic exploitation
10 yrs racialized anxiety
3 yrs of outrage
20 yrs commitment   *20 yrs grace*
20 yrs patience   *20 yrs humour*
20 yrs of triumphs   *20-yrs love*
I Know Rivers......................................*56*
I Love to Write...............................*51*
On Becoming Afro-American..................*53*

1. Place all ingredients in full view

2. Note,.some packaged ingredients are very heavy, others can explode or implode if not handled properly.

3. With strengthening rhythms of drums or the mellowing notes of jazz, gently, carefully loosen the 20 year seals and wrappings on racism, sexism, exploitation and anxiety using lots of commitment, and by reading *I Know Rivers* Part II.

4. Throw away rusted seals, old cartons and any contents that turned sour or spoiled by reading *I Know Rivers* Part III.

5. Place the contents, the core of racism, sexism, exploitation and anxiety in the intellectually controlled refrigerator.

Keep them at about room temperature where they are more useful in analysis, strategic planning and healing. while reading *I Love to Write* (Part I)
Breathe deeply..

6. Pick a variety of greens and feel their freshness and resilence as you wash away some of the harsh and hurtful memories of lynchings and other cruel acts of discrimination. while reading *I Love to Write* (Part II).

7. Arrange some of the greens on a platter and seaon with lots of grace, love and humour while reading *I Love to Write* (Part III).

8 Steam the collard greens with hot water heated by years of outrage until they turn into courage greens while reading *On Becoming an Afro-American* (Parts I & II). Breathe slowly and deeply.

9. Arrange leafy greens around cooked courage greens and sprinkle with memories of triumph and love.and place on a joyfully sparkling serving dish while reading *On Becoming an Afro-American* (Part IV).

10. Serve and eat with strength and resolve and with gestures of freedom and new energy.while reading *On Becoming an Afro-American* (Part V).

11. Prepare, relish serve and eat twice daily for at least 4 months or until recalling particular phrases bring you strength and visions wherever and whenever you need them.

About the author
****

Dr. Olaoye recieved her Ph.D. in 1981 in psychology and has taught psychology for over twenty years at Brookdale Community College and over twelve years as an adjunct at Medgar Evers College, or John Jay College, C.U.N.Y. Dr, Olaoye's area of speciality is Stress and Divesity management. Dr. Olaoye appeared on NBC on Frank Field's Stress and Distress series a fewyears ago and on Storer Cable's Women;s Roundtable with Dr. Amy Handlin. Dr. Olaoye has also conducted numerous poetry readings and workshops: The Log , Williams College, B.Smith;s Rooftop Cafe, New York, Performing Arts Center 101, Brookdale Community College, Barnes & Nable Poetry Series, Ledgewood, N.J.,Historical and Archaological Society of Antigua, Antigua. Additionally, Dr. Olaoye has appeared on Poetry-in-the-Morning, WNYE, The Poet's Corner, WFDU and Antigua Broadcasting Station, ABS TV.

Dr. Olaoye is interested in the role of poetry in the development of the individual and the society as well as poetry as an art form. She is currently exploring various ways in which poetry can be used to help cope with stress and diversity. Dr. Olaoye conducts Stress Management Workshops in which she incorporates the beauty and powerof poetry.

Acknowledgements
✸✸✸✸✸✸✸✸✸

Writing poetry is often a solitary experience, but in conducting poetry readings and workshops there are those who have supported my work and whose encouragements puntuate this volume: Alexander Barton, Actor/Educator, Medgar Evers College who with his awesome baritone voice has enriched my readings for the last five years. Dr. Leo Thorne, Fairleigh Dickinson University, for 13 years of the John Donne Poetry Group at Riverside Church. Dr. Gerry Smith-Wright, Drew Univeristy for co-hosting the monthly Barnes & Noble poetry workshops. Frank Valentino for his dedication to poetry. My colleagues, Susan Rosenberg, Brookdale Community College, for her editorial services and Joel Morgovosky, Franklyn Rother and Teresa Kneuer for their continued support. Dr. Lewis R. Gordon and Dr. Paget Henry, Brown University and Ambassador Patrick Lewis for their reviews of this volume. Thanks also to Cynthia Kaiser for her sales and marketing skills. In Antigua, Dr. George M. Roberts and Michele Henry, Executive Director, Museum of Antigua and Barbuda sponsored poetry readings. To all who helped, my audiences and the new lovers of poetry, thank you! This collection is for you.

STUDENTS' RESPONSES TO USING THE TWO EPISTEMOLOGIES

1. "The poem 'Angry One' (p.42) can provide for a good basic understanding of homeostatis by examination of it in the specific context of emotion. Homeostatic principles underline everything that happens through the progression of the poem."

2. "Zimbardo (2000) defines friendship...as being characterized by intimacy but not by passion and committment... 'Join me after dusk' (p.31) uses several literary devices to get its point across. One of which is metaphor. The poem utilizes nature as a comparison to friendship. The imagery of the hibiscus opening and closing symbolizes the new beginnings friendship provides. Its fading beauty allows us to realize that the "gifts of life" are delicate and may not persevere forever. We must work on our relationships and as in the poem we must "renew" them..'Join me after dusk' describes friendship on a more personal level than Zimbardo."

3. "The principles maintained in 'To look at Anyone' (p. 25) complement those of Attribution Theory...it would be most ideal if all the aspirations in the poem were reachable; but its worth is recognized. Attribution Theory is the extremely watered-down mundane version of the sentiment reflected by the poem."

4. "According to Zick Rubin (1973) there are many objective behaviors that signify love, one of which is the amount of time lovers spend looking in each other's eyes. This aspect of observation becomes for psychologists a means of identifying love.. The triangular theory of love (Sternberg) states that there are three components of love...passion, intimacy and commitment. However, as we shift towards the extensive thoughts on love provided by 'Nyack in moonlit winter' (p. 37, *Passions of the Soul*) the shortfalls of Zimbardo's approach and reasoning are revealed...Elements such as the moonlight waves, wind, snow, fir trees and references to 'taste of earth' establish a relationship betweeen the feelings of the

poet and Nature. It endorses the idea that love is a natural emotion and can be influenced by our natural enviroment...The tone of the poem suggests inner joy, inner peace and a spiritual appreciation for their environment... Once again psychology in its scientific approach has failed to provide a visionary meaning of love. The poem, on the other hand, appeals to the senses of its readers thus allowing them to imagine just what love feels like for them...both approaches tend to complement rather than contradict each other."

****

Order Form
Postal Orders:
Dr. Elaine Olaoye
NorthWest Enterprises
415 East 85th Street, Suite 1G
New York, N.Y. 10028-6354
Fax: 973-770-4748

Name_____
Address_____**City**_
_____
State_____ ____**Zip**_____
Telephone ( )_____
____copies of **Passions of the Soul** at $10.95 **each.**
Tax: Please **add 8 1/4%** sales tax to books shipped to **New York** addresses.
Shipping: $3.00 for first book
                 $1.00 each for additional
Payment: ___Check ___Money Order
Amount enclosed: $_____